20TH CENTURY music

1970s

TURBULENT TIMES

Please visit our web site at: www.garethstevens.com
For a free color catalog describing Gareth Stevens Publishing's list of high-quality books
and multimedia programs, call 1-800-542-2595 or fax your request to (414) 332-3567

Library of Congress Cataloging-in-Publication Data

Hayes, Malcolm.
    1970s: turbulent times / by Malcolm Hayes.
        p. cm. — (20th century music)
    Includes bibliographical references and index.
    Summary: Discusses the influence of people and events worldwide in the 1970s
  which led to developments in minimalism, modern opera and ballet, jazz-rock fusion,
  heavy metal, progressive rock, punk, and reggae.
    ISBN 0-8368-3035-0 (lib. bdg.)
    1. Music—20th century—History and criticism—Juvenile literature. [1. Music—20th
  century—History and criticism.] I. Title. II. 20th century music.
  ML3928.H35   2002
  780'.9'04—dc21   2001054224

This North American edition first published in 2002 by
Gareth Stevens Publishing
A World Almanac Education Group Company
330 West Olive Street, Suite 100
Milwaukee, WI 53212 USA

Original edition © 2001 by David West Children's Books. First published in Great Britain
in 2001 by Heinemann Library, Halley Court, Jordan Hill, Oxford OX2 8EJ, a division of Reed
Educational and Professional Publishing Limited. This U.S. edition © 2002 by Gareth Stevens, Inc.
Additional end matter © 2002 by Gareth Stevens, Inc.

Designer: Rob Shone
Editor: James Pickering
Picture Research: Carrie Haines

Gareth Stevens Editor: Jim Mezzanotte

Photo Credits:
Abbreviations: (t) top, (m) middle, (b) bottom, (l) left, (r) right

Mike Evans/Lebrecht Collection: page 27(b).
David Farrell/Lebrecht Collection: pages 9(t), 10(m), 26(tr).
Betty Freeman/Lebrecht Collection: pages 4(m), 6(b), 11(tl), 12(m, bl), 12-13(t), 13(tr),
    26(bl), 27(mr).
Hulton Getty: pages 6(t), 7(m, b), 10(b).
IRCAM/Lebrecht Collection: page 8(b).
The Kobal Collection: page 4(t).
S. Lauterwasser/Lebrecht Collection: page 8(t).
Lebrecht Collection: page 11(br).
Nigel Luckhurst/Lebrecht Collection: pages 28(both), 29(tr).
Suzie Maeder/Lebrecht Collection: page 7(t).
George Newson/Lebrecht Collection: pages 9(b), 11(tr).
Redferns: cover (m) (Ian Dickson); pages 5(b), 18(mr), 20(both), 21(mr), 23(b) (Michael Ochs
    Archive); 3, 14(t), 19(ml, br), 21(r), 24(b), 25(all) (David Redfern); 19(tr), 22(t), 23(tl, mr) (Richie
    Aaron); 14(b), 15(t, b) (Fin Costello); 17(br), 22(b), 24(l) (Gems); 4(b) (Crixpix); 13(b) (Mick Gold);
    15(m) (Mick Hutson); 16(t) (Dave Ellis); 16(m) (Max Redfern); 16(b) (Glenn A. Baker Archive);
    17(l) (Debi Doss); 18(bl) (A. Putler); 21(tl) (RB).
Rex Features: page 5(t).
Jonathan Smith/Lebrecht Collection: cover (br), page 29(l).
Richard H. Smith/Lebrecht Collection: page 27(tl).
Horst Tappe/Lebrecht Collection: page 9(m).

Printed in the United States of America

1 2 3 4 5 6 7 8 9 06 05 04 03 02

20TH CENTURY music
1970s

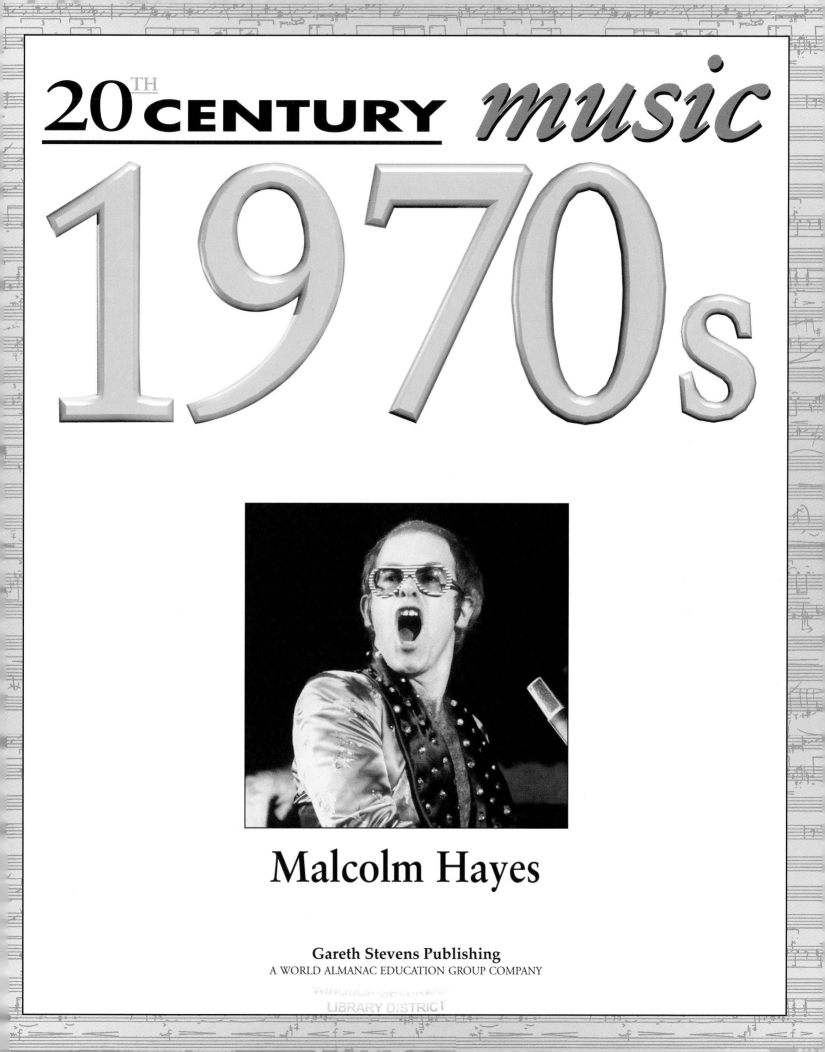

Malcolm Hayes

Gareth Stevens Publishing
A WORLD ALMANAC EDUCATION GROUP COMPANY

CONTENTS

THE END OF INNOCENCE 5

POLITICS THROUGH MUSIC 6

EXOTIC WORLDS 8

AMERICAN INDIVIDUALISTS 10

MINIMALISM 12

HEAVY ROCK 14

PROGRESSIVE ROCK 16

JAZZ AND FUSION 18

FROM PRESLEY TO PENTANGLE 20

RAGE AND RESISTANCE 22

THE SONGWRITERS 24

FROM BIRTWISTLE TO TIPPETT 26

THE END OF AN ERA 28

TIME LINE 30

GLOSSARY 31

BOOKS AND WEB SITES 31

INDEX 32

In the 1970s, Barbra Streisand (b. 1942) had both film and music careers, sometimes writing her own songs. Striesand's albums include The Owl and the Pussycat *(1971),* Classical Barbra *(1976), and* A Star Is Born *(1976).*

In addition to playing with his own ensemble, Philip Glass (front, right) also composed minimalist operas.

Carole King (b. 1942) became a huge success as a singer-songwriter with the album Tapestry *(1971).*

THE END OF INNOCENCE

In the 1975 film version of The Who's rock opera Tommy (1969), Who members Pete Townsend (left), Keith Moon (center), and John Entwistle (right) perform the song "Pinball Wizard."

In the 1970s, the revolution of the 1960s turned nasty. Countries faced terrorism by radical extremists. Economic and political instability created inflation, causing public unrest. The American people had to deal with the Watergate scandal and the resignation of President Richard Nixon. They also had to come to terms with the Vietnam War, which had cost tens of thousands of American lives but still ended in failure for the United States.

The music of the 1970s reflected the turbulence and disillusionment of the decade. Many people tried to escape through rock music, and a culture of excess developed in the rock world. Rock concerts became huge, theatrical events and were often held in stadiums packed with people. Outside of rock, however, some composers created a stripped-down style of music known as minimalism. The world of politics eventually saw a backlash to the excesses of the 1970s. In 1979, voters in both the United States and Britain chose conservative leaders. For the time being, the revolution was over.

Superstar Bob Marley helped make reggae a major musical force in the world.

POLITICS THROUGH MUSIC

The currents of political change swept through Europe. Italy, for instance, almost became a communist state. Left-wing political movements, such as communism, often met with fierce resistance. Many composers expressed their politics through their music.

In the early 1970s, Nono often used unconventional mixed media. His Y Entonces Comprendió, or And Then He Understood (1970), a tribute to the Cuban revolution, was scored for six female voices and electronic tape. The result was confrontational and colorful.

MUSIC FOR THE REVOLUTION

In the first half of the 1970s, Italian Luigi Nono (1924–1990) carried on his personal left-wing musical crusade. *Como una Ola de Fuerza y Luz*, or *Like a Wave of Fire and Light* (1972), for soprano, piano, orchestra, and electronic tape, is a tibute to a leftist hero in Chilea. In the mid-1970s, however, the tone of Nono's music began to change. *Sofferte Onde Serene*, or *Serene Waves Suffered* (1976), for piano and tape, and *Con Luigi Dallapiccola*, or *With Luigi Dallapiccola* (1979), for six percussionists and live electronics, are nonpolitical works written in memory of friends. Luigi Dallapiccola (1904–1975) was one of Italy's major twentieth-century composers.

MUSICAL NONCONFORMIST

American Frederic Rzewski (*b*. 1938) is a classical composer and pianist who also has worked with jazz musicians. His left-wing political stance is apparent in *Coming Together* (1972), which sets to music the words of an inmate at the 1971 uprising in New York's Attica Prison. *Winsboro Cotton Mill Blues* (1979) is based on a 1930s song about working at a North Carolina mill.

Since the mid-1960s, Rzewski has worked frequently in Europe.

HENZE GOES TO CUBA

German Hans Werner Henze (*b.* 1926) was also committed to a left-wing political view, which deepened after his first visit to communist Cuba in 1969 to 1970. His *El Cimarrón* (1970), for baritone singer and three players, is a story about a Cuban runaway slave set in the nineteenth century. Henze also wrote pieces for symphony orchestras. *Heliogabalus Imperator* (1972) is a magnificent symphonic poem about a corrupt emperor in ancient Rome.

Henze's work of the 1970s blended harsh confrontation with alluring sound. His experiences in Cuba led him to add the sounds of Latin American percussion to his music.

Luciano Berio skillfully balanced the aggressiveness of his music with the need to be accessible to audiences.

RADICAL POLITICS, RADICAL ATTITUDE

The music of Italian Luciano Berio (*b.* 1925) was not so strongly leftist but still expressed leftist themes. His stage work *Opera* (1970) explored what he saw as the decline of both opera and the middle class society that created it. *Coro* (1976), for chorus and orchestra, used leftist and folk texts.

Separating communist East Berlin from noncommunist West Berlin, the Berlin Wall symbolized a deeply divided European continent. East Germans who tried to escape over the wall to the West were usually shot by East German guards.

EXOTIC WORLDS

In the 1970s, the heroes of the avant-garde all pursued their own agendas. Some expanded and refined their existing personal styles. Others kept searching for new sounds and new ways of creating them.

IRCAM gave Pierre Boulez a new outlet for his belief in the radical possibilities of music's future. This center in Paris was created for him with the personal support of French president Georges Pompidou.

SOUNDS OF THE FUTURE

Frenchman Pierre Boulez (*b.* 1925) and German Karlheinz Stockhausen (*b.* 1928) had once been close colleagues, but they were now following different musical paths. Boulez did most of his work at IRCAM (Institut de Recherche et Coordination Acoustique/Musique), where he and other composers explored the possibilities of computer-generated sound. Stockhausen, meanwhile, created *Trans* (1971), for instruments and electronic tape, and *Inori* (1974), for orchestra, both of which were semi-theatrical works that incorporated elements of rock.

Ever since the electronic experiments of the 1950s, composers had been aware of the almost unlimited possibilities for transforming traditional musical sounds or generating entirely new ones. The purpose of IRCAM was to channel these possibilities in a creative direction. This blueprint shows a layout of IRCAM and its equipment.

le bâtiment et ses équipements

ESPACE DE PROJECTION STUDIO REGIE LOCAL STOCKAGE CHAMBRE SOURDE STUDIO D'ENREGISTREMENT AVEC REGIE STUDIOS COUPE SUR L'ESPACE DE PROJECTION

MESSIAEN'S CANYONS

The works of French composer Olivier Messiaen (1908–1992) glorified both his Catholic faith and what he considered its purest image in nature — the songs of birds. A visit to Utah's Bryce Canyon inspired *Des Canyons aux Etoiles*, or *From the Canyons to the Stars* (1974), a huge, twelve-movement work for solo piano, horn, and orchestra.

Menuhin with violin and Shankar with sitar

EXPRESSION AND MORE ADVENTURE

Toru Takemitsu (1930–1996) was the leading voice among Japanese composers. His orchestral work *A Flock Descends into the Pentagonal Garden* (1977) is a beautiful expression of the oriental spirit through western musical media. Hungarian György Ligeti (*b*. 1923) pursued adventurous experiments in theatre and sound, particularly in his witty and outrageous opera *Le Grand Macabre* (1978). Ligeti's major instrumental works include *Clocks and Clouds* (1973), for chorus and orchestra.

RAVI SHANKAR AND YEHUDI MENUHIN

Ravi Shankar (*b*. 1920) has made it his mission to bring Indian classical music to audiences in the West, so he has collaborated with Western musicians. He found a kindred spirit in the celebrated American violinist Yehudi Menuhin (1916–1999), who was also deeply interested in Indian culture, history, tradition, and thought.

9

György Ligeti found a way to combine both spontaneity and precision in his music. These qualities can be heard in his Double Concerto (1972), for flute, oboe, and orchestra.

Because of his interest in creating straightforwardly beautiful sounds, Takemitsu and his music were a welcome presence at Western musical events, such as the Aldeburgh Festival in Suffolk, England.

AMERICAN INDIVIDUALISTS

The finest of America's older, established composers refused to follow trends around them. They forged their own musical paths, however unfashionable. The music of Conlon Nancarrow (1912–1997), a gifted American composer who spent years in obscurity, began to find a wider audience.

BERNSTEIN GROWS AND EXPLORES

Leonard Bernstein (1918–1990), while busy as a world famous conductor, composed a ballet, *Dybbuk* (1974), and an orchestral song cycle, *Songfest* (1977). Bernstein's semi-theatrical work *Mass* (1971) was a mixed success, as was *1600 Pennsylvania Avenue*. This musical, with lyrics by Alan Jay Lerner, was composed for the U.S. Bicentennial in 1976. It portrays a series of U.S. presidents and first ladies through the ages.

UNIQUE TALENT

American Conlon Nancarrow settled in Mexico City in 1940. In the late 1940s, he began creating brilliantly inventive studies for player-piano. He composed the music by punching holes in the piano's paper rolls, creating fantastically complex rhythms. In the 1970s, when some of these player-piano studies were published and recorded, Nancarrow began to recieve more recognition for his work.

Some of Bernstein's greatest successes as a conductor were with European orchestras, most notably the Vienna Philharmonic.

Bernstein and Carter both contributed important works for the 1976 U.S. Bicentennial celebration.

Nancarrow had studied classical music, but he also played jazz trumpet. Both influences shaped the rhythmic strength of his music.

Carter renewed his interest in vocal works in the 1970s, but he also finished his Third String Quartet (1971) and Duo for Violin and Piano (1974).

CARTER: SYMPHONIES AND SONG CYCLES

By the 1970s, Elliott Carter (*b*. 1908) was an elder statesman of modernism. His complex Symphony of Three Orchestras (1976) was commissioned for the 1976 U.S. Bicentennial. Carter also composed two song cycles based on texts by American poets — *A Mirror on Which to Dwell* (1975), with words by Elizabeth Bishop, and *Syringa* (1978), with words by John Ashbery.

Crumb has said that his music draws on the natural sounds and acoustics he "inherited" from the hills of Charleston, West Virginia, where he was born.

MUSIC OF CHILDREN AND ANGELS

George Crumb (*b*. 1929) became internationally famous in the 1970s through two dark and powerful chamber works, each drawing together a remarkable range of sounds and musical styles. His song cycle *Ancient Voices of Children* (1970) sets to music words by Spanish poet Federico García Lorca, while *Black Angels* (1970) is for an amplified string quartet in which members also play percussion instruments. In 1971, Crumb followed with another atmospheric chamber work called *Vox Balaenae*, or *Voice of the Whale*, based on the recorded "singing" of humpback whales.

MINIMALISM

Minimalism has been around for centuries. Composers as diverse as Beethoven, Wagner, and Sibelius used repeated and overlapping melodic and rhythmic patterns as an effective musical device. In the 1970s, minimalist composers built entire works this way.

PHILIP GLASS

In addition to performing instrumental works with his own ensemble, American Philip Glass (*b.* 1937) also wrote two operas. *Einstein on the Beach* (1976) was a collaboration with the theater director Robert Wilson, while *Satyagraha* (1979) portrays the early life of Mahatma Gandhi and Gandhi's philosophy of nonviolent political resistance. Glass's music is generally more driving and insistent than the music of Steve Reich or John Adams.

Glass (front, right) *in rehearsal*

Minimalist music's apparent simplicity often disguises how demanding it can be to perform. Navigating its gradual changes and intricate patterns requires exceptionally strong nerves and concentration. Steve Reich tackled the problem by starting his own ensemble.

PHASES AND PATTERNS

American Steve Reich (*b.* 1936) formed his own ensemble to play his minimalist music, which includes the works *Drumming* (1971), *Music for Mallet Instruments, Voices and Organ* (1973), and *Music for Eighteen Musicians* (1976). Influenced by African drumming and Balinese gamelan music, these works first establish overlapping musical patterns, then gradually shift them out of phase with each other to form new patterns. Americans Terry Riley (*b.* 1935) and La Monte Young (*b.* 1935) explored similar musical territory in their own individual ways.

Terry Riley (seated) *explored overlapping musical patterns with electronic keyboards on* The Persian Surgery Dervishes (1972), *which also showed his interest in Indian music.*

La Monte Young developed his concept of drone-based music while studying with Karlheinz Stockhausen. He has performed his music with light shows devised by his wife, artist Marian Zazeela.

A NEW TALENT

Another American, John Adams (*b.* 1947), first became interested in electronic music, then, influenced by Reich and others, began to develop a different style of composing. This new style combined minimalism's intricate pattern-making with the long-range harmonic reach of the classical symphonic tradition. *Shaker Loops* (1978) marked Adams's arrival as a major talent.

TUBULAR BELLS SELLS

In 1973, Mike Oldfield (*b.* 1953) released the instrumental album *Tubular Bells* on Virgin Records, a new label owned by a record retailer named Richard Branson. Nineteen-year-old Oldfield, from England, played most of the instruments himself on this minimalist rock album. He also conducted an orchestral arrangement of the work. The album went on to sell sixteen million copies. Its huge success made Oldfield, Branson, and Virgin Records famous.

Classically trained Riley and Young found that their music had an influence on rock, but in Oldfield's case, rock influenced the classical world. In 1975, avant-garde composer David Bedford (b. 1937) released an orchestral arrangement of Tubular Bells.

HEAVY ROCK

In the 1960s, an explosive blues-based rock music was pioneered by groups such as Cream and the Jimi Hendrix Experience. In the 1970s, this kind of rock music flourished, becoming even louder, heavier, and more confrontational.

LOUDER THAN CLASSICAL

In 1973, the British rock group Deep Purple was credited in the *Guinness Book of Records* as being the world's loudest band. Deep Purple's music blended the heavy rock style of guitarist Ritchie Blackmore with the classical influences of keyboard player Jon Lord. The group's albums include *Deep Purple in Rock* (1970), *Machine Head* (1972), and the live double album *Made in Japan* (1973).

Robert Plant (left) *and Jimmy Page of Led Zeppelin perform in their 1970s heyday.*

LED ZEPPELIN

The British group Led Zeppelin dominated rock in the 1970s almost as completely as the Beatles did in the 1960s. With such albums as *Led Zeppelin III* (1970), the unnamed fourth album (1971), and *Physical Graffiti* (1975), the band's style ranged from thunderously heavy blues to gentler folk, all of it driven by Jimmy Page's dazzling guitar playing and Robert Plant's powerful, shrill-to-soft vocals.

Deep Purple traveled in their own Boeing 720 airliner, which was called Starship I.

15

Guitarist Tony Iommi (left) and vocalist Ozzy Osbourne (right) led the British rock band Black Sabbath to fame and notoriety.

Even in the 1970s, performing with a live boa constrictor was a "far-out" idea, but Alice Cooper did it. The snake's name was Angela.

WILDER SHORES

The pounding, ear-shattering world of heavy metal was dominated by groups whose stage shows were as deliberately outrageous as the noise level of their music. England's Black Sabbath was hugely successful on both sides of the Atlantic with its albums *Black Sabbath* and *Paranoid* (both 1970), and *Master of Reality* (1971). The American band Alice Cooper, whose lead singer eventually adopted the same name, was notorious for the flamboyant theatrics of its stage shows. The group's albums *School's Out* (1972) and *Billion Dollar Babies* (1973) sold in the millions.

TAKING ON THE WORLD

Formed in New York City in 1972, the band Kiss eventually found huge success in the United States and abroad. Taking the theatrics of Alice Cooper several steps further, Kiss members adopted cartoonlike costumes and makeup. While Kiss might not have appealed to older, more conservative listeners, the group's music and antics were a hit with teenage America. The most successful Kiss albums include *Alive* (1975), *Destroyer* and *Rock and Roll Over* (both 1976), and *Love Gun* (1977).

By the late 1970s, Kiss had achieved massive commercial success with its theatrical brand of rock and roll.

PROGRESSIVE ROCK

By the 1970s, rock music had traveled far from its roots. Rock musicians explored new territory, often incorporating classical influences and virtuoso playing. The era's elaborate concerts reflected rock music's new ambitions.

Ian Anderson composes, sings, and plays the flute.

16

Yes concerts were often magical events for Yes fans, who flocked to hear music from this group's albums, such as Tales from Topographic Oceans *(1973) and* Relayer *(1974).*

Vocalist, guitarist, and bassist Greg Lake (left), drummer Carl Palmer (center), and keyboardist Keith Emerson drew on a variety of classical and rock influences.

CLASSICAL PROGRESS

On albums such as *Fragile* (1971) and *Close to the Edge* (1972), the British band Yes featured the keyboard work of classically trained Rick Wakeman. Keyboardist Keith Emerson, of the British group Emerson, Lake and Palmer, or "ELP," also had classical training. ELP's 1972 albums *Tarkus* and *Pictures at an Exhibition* ambitiously fused rock and classical elements.

STAYING POWER

Jethro Tull is named after an eighteenth century agriculturist. The group features songwriter and vocalist Ian Anderson, who also plays the flute. Anderson first began playing flute after listening to jazz multi-instrumentalist Rahsaan Roland Kirk. Jethro Tull had success with albums such as *Aqualung* (1971) and *Thick as a Brick* (1972). The group still performs and records today.

PROGRESSIVE ROCK THRIVES

Genesis was started by schoolmates at the Charterhouse public school in England. The group made its mark with such albums as *Foxtrot* (1972) and *Selling England by the Pound* (1973). After songwriter and lead singer Peter Gabriel left in 1975, Phil Collins, the group's drummer, took over as vocalist. The Moody Blues, who were also from England, refined the orchestral rock they had pioneered in the 1960s on *Seventh Sojourn* (1972). In 1973, the British band Pink Floyd released *Dark Side of the Moon*, one of the best selling albums of all time.

THE ART OF SELF-INVENTION

Born David Jones in 1947, British rocker David Bowie achieved stardom by personifying characters he invented on albums such as *The Rise and Fall of Ziggy Stardust and the Spiders from Mars* (1972) and *Aladdin Sane* (1973). He also produced albums for American rockers Iggy Pop (*b.* James Osterburg, 1947) and Lou Reed (*b.* 1942) and collaborated with Brian Eno (*b.* 1948), former keyboardist for the British group Roxy Music, on the album *Low* (1977).

David Bowie's provocative changes of image and musical personality encompassed his albums Diamond Dogs *(1974),* Station to Station *(1976), and* Heroes *(1977).*

The allure of Lou Reed's songs in Berlin *(1973) and* Coney Island Baby *(1976) is offset by an inner bleakness.*

JAZZ AND FUSION

Like their rock counterparts, jazz musicians in the 1970s experimented with blending together different kinds of music. Fusion jazz mixed the progressive jazz of the 1960s with rock and even classical music.

MILES RETIRES WHILE OTHERS CARRY ON

American jazz trumpeter Miles Davis (1926–1991) continued his 1960s pursuit of jazz-rock fusion in the 1970s with albums such as *A Tribute to Jack Johnson* (1970), before a car crash and illness sidelined him for several years. In 1970, two musicians who played with Davis, American saxophonist Wayne Shorter (*b.* 1933) and Austrian-born keyboardist Joe Zawinul (*b.* 1932), founded Weather Report, which became one of the decade's foremost fusion bands.

ULTIMATE PIANIST

A child prodigy, American pianist Keith Jarrett (*b.* 1945) always had an interest in playing both jazz and classical music. Besides collaborating with musicians such as Miles Davis and drummer Art Blakey, Jarrett has performed solo concerts that are legendary for their brilliant improvisation. *The Köln Concert* (1975) is a live recording that captures some of that brilliance.

18

"Changing from day to day like the weather" is how Joe Zawinul (far left) described the music of Weather Report, a group he founded with Wayne Shorter (second from left).

STAR PIANISTS

When American Chick Corea (*b.* 1941) formed the fusion group Return to Forever, in 1971, he was already a renowned keyboardist who had worked with Miles Davis and other jazz greats. Return to Forever was considerably successful throughout the decade. Oscar Peterson (*b.* 1925), from Canada, performed mostly as a solo pianist after 1970, dazzling audiences with his technique.

JAZZ GOES EAST

Influenced by Indian philosophy and music, British guitarist John McLaughlin (*b.* 1942) founded the Mahavishnu Orchestra in 1971 with American drummer Billy Cobham (*b.* 1944). Two of the band's finest albums are *The Inner Mounting Flame* (1971) and *Birds of Fire* (1972). McLaughlin also teamed up with the California rock group Santana in 1973. Two years later, Cobham formed a new group, Spectrum. U.S. native Freddie Hubbard (*b.* 1938) played trumpet and flugelhorn with various fusion groups. In 1977 he formed the "hard bop" band V.S.O.P. with Wayne Shorter.

Chick Corea contributed his skills as a keyboardist and composer to the group Return to Forever, whose albums include Light as a Feather (1972).

19

Freddie Hubbard excelled on the trumpet and on its mellow, buglelike cousin, the flugelhorn. With Wayne Shorter, he founded the group V.S.O.P.

The mastery of Oscar Peterson descends from such legendary jazz pianists as Erroll Garner (1923–1977) and Art Tatum (1909–1956).

FROM PRESLEY TO PENTANGLE

Rock music of the 1970s overlapped with folk, country, and blues, so a wide variety of music now fell under the "rock" label. The decade's best groups each created a unique sound, and a legendary rock-and-roll original continued a triumphant comeback.

STILL THE KING

In the late 1960s, when his rise to stardom in the 1950s seemed a distant memory, Elvis Presley (1935–1977) staged a remarkable comeback. He continued to regain his star status in the 1970s with songs such as "The Wonder of You" (1970) and "Burning Love" (1972). He also made the films *Elvis – That's The Way It Is* (1970) and *Elvis on Tour* (1973).

Although his health declined rapidly in the 1970s, Elvis never lost his talent.

The Fleetwood Mac of the 1970s barely resembled the original 1960s version, which was a blues band.

MEGASTAR MAC

Fleetwood Mac was born in the 1960s as a British blues band. After moving from London to California and adding two U.S. natives, Stevie Nicks and Lindsay Buckingham, the group became one of the ultimate rock acts of the 1970s. For several years, *Rumours* (1977) was the biggest-selling album of all time. It sold twenty-five million copies. *Tusk* (1979) was another epic success.

Despite their many personality clashes, musicians (from left to right) Nash, Crosby, Young, and Stills created some brilliant music.

Hotel California *was a huge hit for the Eagles, but they recorded many other successful albums, including* On the Border *(1974),* One of These Nights *(1975), and* The Long Run *(1979).*

ROCK MEETS COUNTRY AND FOLK

The California-based Eagles found success in the 1970s with their country-influenced rock, which became harder-edged as the decade progressed. Their albums *Desperado* (1973) and *Hotel California* (1976) sold millions. Crosby, Stills, and Nash featured gentler folk-influenced vocal harmonies. The California-based trio was occasionally joined by Canadian Neil Young (*b.* 1945), who added a harder edge to *Déjà Vu* (1970) and the live album *Four Way Street* (1971).

BRITISH FOLK MUSIC

In England, the relatively mellow music of Pentangle centered around vocalist Jacqui McShee and two acoustic guitarists, Bert Jansch and John Renbourn. The band recorded *Cruel Sister* (1970) and *Solomon's Seal* (1972). Fairport Convention had a heavier sound, with electric guitar and the powerful fiddle playing of Dave Swarbrick. Lead vocalist Sandy Denny left the group before *Full House* (1970) and *Angel Delight* (1971), but returned for *Rising for the Moon* (1975).

Pentangle members, (from left to right) John Renbourn, Danny Thompson, Jacqui McShee, Terry Cox, and Bert Jansch perform their stylish and elegant brand of folk.

RAGE AND RESISTANCE

The turmoil and dissatisfaction of the 1970s found many different outlets in popular music. In England, punk rock challenged mainstream rock's self-indulgent excess with short, simple songs driven by a relentless beat, capturing the era's anger and aggression. New York City became a center for some new kinds of music. On the Caribbean island of Jamaica, reggae emerged with a potent blend of infectious rhythms and social commentary.

Sid Vicious (left) and Johnny Rotten did not attempt to charm their audiences.

SOUND AND FURY

The Sex Pistols were arguably the most notorious punk band. They started out in London in 1975 and disbanded three years later, after a stormy American tour, the departure of lead vocalist Johnny Rotten (John Lydon), and the death of bassist Sid Vicious (John Ritchie). They managed to offend a lot of people with their behavior and music, which had been their intention. Other British bands, such as the Clash, joined the 1970s punk rebellion.

With its bright, bouncy sound, the New York band Blondie found success in 1978 with "Sunday Girl" and "Heart of Glass."

22

Formed in 1974, the Ramones were America's hard-hitting counterpart to the Sex Pistols.

AMERICA'S NEW SOUNDS

In New York City, the Ramones were playing punk with the same angry abandon as the Sex Pistols, but Blondie, also from New York, had a friendlier sound. Fronted by singer Debbie Harry (*b*. 1945), Blondie was part of 1970s New York's "new wave" of fresh talent and attitude. The group was a wild success on both sides of the Atlantic.

CARIBBEAN CHARISMA

With its laid-back but insistent rhythmic sound, reggae developed in Jamaica as a musical symbol of black self-affirmation. Reggae's international superstar was Bob Marley (1945–1981). During a violent general election campaign in 1978, Marley invited Jamaica's two leading political opponents, Michael Manley and Edward Seaga, to appear together on stage with him, in a gesture of reconciliation. Neither politician dared to refuse.

HEADS ARE TALKING

Talking Heads started in New York in 1975, led by singer-songwriter David Byrne (*b*. 1952). More new wave than punk, their angry-yet-arty songs still appealed to punk audiences. The group's two best-selling albums were *More Songs About Buildings and Food* (1978) and *Fear of Music* (1979).

23

David Byrne (center) *performs with Chris Frantz* (left) *and Tina Weymouth.*

Bob Marley's stardom helped turn reggae into a musical and political symbol of Afro-Caribbean individuality and self-reliance.

THE SONGWRITERS

The best songwriters change with the times they live in, yet remain true to themselves. In the 1970s, leading songwriters from the 1960s joined talented newcomers in forging new musical expressions.

By the late 1960s, Bob Dylan's cutting blend of folk, rock, and blues had changed to a mellower, country-influenced style. In the mid-1970s, however, Dylan returned to the hard-edged style of his earlier work.

RARE TALENT

Born Roberta Joan Anderson in 1943, Canadian Joni Mitchell was one of the most outstanding singer-songwriters of the 1970s. *Ladies of the Canyon* (1970), with its ballads and bittersweet lyrics, was a breakthrough success. With *Blue* (1971), *Court and Spark* (1974), *The Hissing of Summer Lawns* (1975), and *Hejira* (1976), she pursued her thoughtful blend of folk, rock, and jazz.

Joni Mitchell left Canada to find fame in the United States.

TROUBADOURS OF THEIR TIME

Bob Dylan (*b.* Robert Zimmerman, 1941) brilliantly rediscovered his best, most bitter form with *Blood on the Tracks* and *Desire* (both 1975). Neil Young secured his reputation as a master of both heavy electric and gentler acoustic rock with the solo albums *After the Goldrush* (1970) and *Harvest* (1972). He also performed with Crosby, Stills, and Nash.

"Mull of Kintyre," a tribute by Paul and Linda McCartney (left and center) to their home in western Scotland, featured Wings and the Campbeltown pipe band.

BRITISH SUPERSTARS

The Beatles broke up in 1970. That same year, Paul McCartney (*b.* 1942) released his solo album *McCartney*. It contained one of his best songs, "Maybe I'm Amazed." McCartney then toured and recorded with his group Wings, achieving huge success with *Band on the Run* (1973) and "Mull of Kintyre" (1977). John Lennon (1940–1980) also pursued a successful solo career with the chart-topping album *Imagine* (1971) and subsequent albums *Mind Games* (1973) and *Walls and Bridges* (1974). Elton John (*b.* Reginald Dwight, 1947) built a huge following with his brand of piano-accompanied rock. His double album *Goodbye Yellow Brick Road* (1973) included "Candle in the Wind," a song that he would later adapt for Princess Diana's funeral.

Elton John's Don't Shoot Me I'm Only the Piano Player *topped the British and U.S. album charts in 1973.*

Abba's Eurovision success with "Waterloo" was soon followed by the classic singles "SOS," "Take a Chance on Me," and "The Name of the Game."

SWEDEN'S SUPERSTARS

Abba launched its career by winning the 1974 Eurovision Song Contest. The Swedish group's world acclaim was spurred on by "Mamma Mia," "Chiquitita," and "Dancing Queen." The songwriting talent of Benny Andersson and Bjorn Ulvaeus laid the foundation for Abba's success.

FROM BIRTWISTLE TO TIPPETT

FIn the 1970s, British composers created works that were more sharply individualistic than those of other European composers. One established British figure found some spectacular late success.

POWER AND ATMOSPHERE

Building on his uncompromising style of the 1960s, Harrison Birtwistle (*b*. 1934) became an increasingly major force with his orchestral work *The Triumph of Time* (1972) and some powerful experiments in musical theater, notably *Bow Down* (1977). Peter Maxwell Davies (*b*. 1934) went to live in Scotland's Orkney Islands, the landscapes and atmosphere of which inspired much of his music. *Stone Litany* (1973) was a setting of some local Norse runic inscriptions for mezzo-soprano and orchestra. In 1976, Davies completed his First Symphony.

The Orkney Islands had a deep influence on the music of Peter Maxwell Davies. His opera The Martyrdom of St. Magnus *(1977) tells the story of the islands' patron saint. The sounds of wind and sea inspired* Westerlings *(1976).*

Silbury Hill, a prehistoric English burial mound, gave Harrison Birtwistle the title of his Silbury Air *(1977), for instrumental ensemble. During much of the 1970s, he worked on the opera score* The Mask of Orpheus *(1973–1983).*

SPIRITUAL VALUES

John Tavener (*b.* 1944) explored some musical territory that was quite different from the post-avant-garde world of Birtwistle and Davies. He based his style on the simplicity and power of religious chant, as in the monumental *Ultimos Ritos* (1972). Tavener's *Liturgy of St. John Chrysostom* (1978) is a statement about his conversion to Orthodox Christianity in 1976.

Tavener's conversion to Orthodox Christianity strengthened his belief that composers should convey religious truths beyond our understanding.

THE APPARENTLY AGELESS TIPPETT

The music of Michael Tippett (1905–1998) revealed a fresh creative energy in the 1970s. Tippett's work became widely popular in Britain and the United States, partly because of a successful recording of his earlier opera *The Midsummer Marriage* (1955). Tippet also created two new operas in the 1970s. *The Knot Garden* (1970) is about personality clashes and psychoanalysis. *The Ice Break* (1977) was Tippett's response to the political and racial troubles going on in Britain and the United States during the decade.

INTRICATE INVENTION

Brian Ferneyhough (*b.* 1943) explored a musical style of "new complexity," notated in extreme rhythmic and expressive detail. Ferneyhough's major work of the 1970s was *Transit* (1977), for amplified voices and instrumental ensemble. It was based on a medieval woodcut of a human figure moving across the boundaries separating Heaven and Earth.

Ferneyhough is a master of complex and detailed music.

27

Tippett's opera The Knot Garden *mixed contemporary psychoanalysis with a plot based on Shakespeare's play* The Tempest. *The result was a complex and brilliant score that was influenced by blues and jazz.*

THE END OF AN ERA

For many years, two of the great masters of twentieth-century classical music had shown that "style wars" did not matter when a work had quality and depth. Their deaths in the mid-1970s marked the end of an era.

A HAUNTED SUNSET

The last years of British composer Benjamin Britten (1913–1976) were clouded by illness, yet he was at the height of his creative powers. He composed an opera for television, *Owen Wingrave* (1971), and another, *Death in Venice* (1973), for the Aldeburgh Festival, which he had directed for many years. Britten's cantata *Phaedra* (1975) and his Third String Quartet (1975) were among the finest works he ever wrote.

Britten (left) would have been a different composer without Peter Pears (right), for whose tenor voice he created many of his vocal works. His choice of texts owed much to Pears' extensive knowledge of English literature.

Britten was greatly inspired by the musical qualities of particular artists. His cantata Phaedra *was composed for the great mezzo-soprano Janet Baker. In this rehearsal for the Aldeburgh Festival premiere, Steuart Bedford conducts the English Chamber Orchestra. Janet Baker is behind him, singing.*

SHADOW OF DEATH

Despite suffering several heart attacks, Russian composer Dmitri Shostakovich (1906–1975) wrote a series of somber masterworks in the last years of his life. These works include the last three of his fifteen string quartets (1970–1974); his Fifteenth Symphony (1971), which quotes music by Italian composer Gioacchino Rossini (1792–1868) and German composer Richard Wagner (1813–1883); and a viola sonata (1975).

28

This bust of Shostakovich stands outside his former home in Leningrad (now St. Petersburg). In 1941, he worked at home on his "Leningrad Symphony" while the city was being attacked by the German army.

В ЭТОМ ДОМЕ
ЖИЛ И РАБОТАЛ
С 1937 ПО 1941 Г.
ВЕЛИКИЙ
СОВЕТСКИЙ
КОМПОЗИТОР
ДМИТРИЙ
ДМИТРИЕВИЧ
ШОСТАКОВИЧ
ЗДЕСЬ ИМ СОЗДАВАЛАСЬ
СЕДЬМАЯ
(ЛЕНИНГРАДСКАЯ)
СИМФОНИЯ

Peter Pears (seated) as Gustav von Aschenbach, the principal role in Death in Venice

LATE MASTERPIECE

As his health deteriorated, Benjamin Britten was offered the choice of immediate heart surgery or the riskier option of continuing work on *Death in Venice*. He essentially shortened his life by insisting on finishing the opera first. *Death in Venice* is a dark and beautiful study of fatal emotional obsession. Its leading role was the last major one that Britten wrote for English tenor Peter Pears.

THE COMPOSER SPEAKS — OR DOES HE?

After Shostakovich's death, *Testimony*, a book that was supposedly his ghost-written memoirs, appeared in translation in the West. It portrayed an artist mentally scarred by life under communism, and it contrasted sharply with the image of the proud "official composer" that Soviet officials promoted for years. Today, the book is still denounced by many as a fabrication. With the passage of time, however, as well as the end of the Soviet era, more information about the composer has come out, and a consensus is now forming that the substance of *Testimony* is essentially accurate.

· TIME LINE ·

	WORLD EVENTS	MUSICAL EVENTS	THE ARTS	FAMOUS MUSICIANS	MUSICAL WORKS
1970	• National Guardsmen kill four students at Kent State University in Ohio	• Isle of Wight rock festival in UK	• Robert Altman: M*A*S*H • Death of English writer E. M. Forster	• Deaths of Janis Joplin and Jimi Hendrix • The Beatles split up • Mariah Carey born	• Deep Purple in Rock • Simon and Garfunkel: Bridge over Troubled Water
1971	• First U.S. and Soviet space missions to Mars	• First Queen concert • Benefit concert for people of Bangladesh	• Pablo Neruda wins Nobel Prize for literature	• Deaths of composers Igor Stravinsky and Carl Ruggles	• Joni Mitchell: Blue • Shostakovich: Fifteenth Symphony • John Lennon: Imagine
1972	• Salt I treaty signed by U.S. and USSR	• Film release of Elvis on Tour • Mar Y Sol festival in Puerto Rico	• Francis Ford Coppola: The Godfather	• Carly Simon records "You're So Vain" with Mick Jagger	• Harrison Birtwistle: The Triumph of Time • Freddie Hubbard: First Light
1973	• Last U.S. troops withdraw from Vietnam	• Led Zeppelin concert in Tampa, Florida breaks U.S. box office record ($309,000)	• Death of poet W. H. Auden • Roger Moore stars in Live and Let Die	• Death of cellist Pablo Casals • Death of conductor Otto Klemperer	• Benjamin Britten: Death in Venice • Pink Floyd: Dark Side of the Moon
1974	• U.S. president Nixon resigns over Watergate	• California Jam with Deep Purple, Black Sabbath, and ELP draws 300,000 spectators	• Exile of Russian writer Alexander Solzhenitsyn to the West	• Mick Taylor quits the Rolling Stones	• Olivier Messiaen: Des Canyons aux Etoiles • Stockhausen: Inori • Elton John: Caribou
1975	• End of Vietnam War • Cambodia overrun by Pol Pot's Khmer Rouge	• Keith Jarrett plays The Köln Concert • Film release of The Who's Tommy	• Milos Forman: One Flew over the Cuckoo's Nest • Spielberg: Jaws	• Death of Dmitri Shostakovich • John Lennon retires • Peter Gabriel quits Genesis	• Britten: Phaedra and Third String Quartet • Queen: "Bohemian Rhapsody"
1976	• Death of Chinese leader Mao Tse-tung	• Paul McCartney's first U.S. tour in ten years • Punk sweeps the UK	• Sylvester Stallone stars in Rocky • Death of French writer André Malraux	• Death of Britten • The Clash formed	• Henryk Górecki: Symphony, no. 3 • Led Zeppelin: Presence • Abba: "Dancing Queen"
1977	• UN bans arms sales to South Africa	• Film release of Saturday Night Fever sparks disco craze	• Woody Allen: Annie Hall • Lucas: Star Wars • Premiere of TV series Roots	• Def Leppard formed • Deaths of Elvis Presley and opera soprano Maria Callas	• Fleetwood Mac: Rumours • Michael Tippett: The Ice Break
1978	• Karol Wojtyla becomes Pope John Paul II	• Peter Maxwell Davies's First Symphony first performed	• Isaac Bashevis Singer wins Nobel Prize for literature	• David Coverdale forms Whitesnake • Death of The Who's drummer, Keith Moon	• Carter: Syringa • Kate Bush: "Wuthering Heights" • Grease soundtrack
1979	• Margaret Thatcher becomes Britain's first woman prime minister	• Led Zeppelin records its final album	• William Styron: Sophie's Choice • Francis Ford Coppola: Apocalypse Now	• Deaths of jazz bassist Charles Mingus and American composer Roy Harris	• Glass: Satyagraha • The Police: Outlandos d'Amour

GLOSSARY

avant-garde: an artistic movement that developed experimental styles to challenge tradition.

baritone: a male singing voice with a low to middle range, or a musical instrument with a similar range.

cantata: a musical work composed for a chorus.

chamber music: instrumental music written for a small group of musicians, intended to be performed in a room or small concert hall.

concerto: a musical work for a solo instrument and an orchestra, written in three different movements.

gamelan: an Indonesian orchestra that uses mostly percussion instruments, such as drums, gongs, and xylophones.

hard bop: a more aggressive form of bop, which is a jazz style involving complex melody, harmony, and rhythm.

mezzo-soprano: a female singing voice with a range just below soprano, which is the highest range.

modernism: an artistic philosophy and practice that seeks to break with traditions of the past and find new forms of expression.

setting: music composed for some kind of text, such as a poem.

sonata: a musical work composed for one or more solo instruments.

study: an instrumental work, especially for piano, written to explore a particular aspect of performing and composing technique.

tenor: a male singing voice with a middle-to-high range, or a musical instrument with a similar range.

troubadour: a traveling singer-songwriter in medieval Italy and France.

MORE BOOKS TO READ

Barbra Streisand. Women of Achievement (series). Rita Pappas (Chelsea House)

Bob Marley. They Died Too Young (series). Millie Gilfoyle (Chelsea House)

Elvis Presley. People Who Made History (series). James D. Torr, editor (Greenhaven Press)

Jazz: An American Saga. James Lincoln Collier (Henry Holt & Company)

Led Zeppelin: In Their Own Words. Paul Kendall and Dave Lewis (Omnibus)

Leonard Bernstein: A Passion for Music. Johanna Hurwitz (Jewish Publication Society)

Miles Davis. Black Americans of Achievement (series). Ron Frankl (Chelsea House)

One Love, One Heart: A History of Reggae. James Haskins (Jump at the Sun)

WEB SITES

György Ligeti.
www.sonyclassical.com/artists/ligeti_bio.htm

The Folk Musician: Bob Dylan. *www.time.com/time/time100/artists/profile/dylan.html*

Music on the Web: Benjamin Britten (1913–1976).
www.musicweb.uk.net/britten

Ravi Shankar.
www.ravishankar.org/bio.html

A Tribute to Oscar Peterson.
www.oscarpeterson.com/op

Philip Glass.
www.philipglass.com

Due to the dynamic nature of the Internet, some web sites stay current longer than others. To find additional web sites, use a reliable search engine with one or more of the following keywords: *Elliott Carter, Chick Corea, Keith Jarrett, Olivier Messiaen, Joni Mitchell, Conlon Nancarrow, Steve Reich, Dimitri Shostakovich,* and *Michael Tippett.*

INDEX

1600 Pennsylvania Avenue 10

Abba 25
Adams, John 12, 13
Alice Cooper 15
Ancient Voices of Children 11

Baker, Janet 28
Berio, Luciano 7
Bernstein, Leonard 10
Birtwistle, Harrison 26, 27
Black Angels 11
Black Sabbath 15
Blakey, Art 18
Blondie 22, 23
Boulez, Pierre 8
Bow Down 26
Bowie, David 17
Britten, Benjamin 28, 29
Byrne, David 23

Carter, Elliott 10, 11
Cimarrón, El 7
Clash 22
Clocks and Clouds 9
Cobham, Billy 19
Coming Together 6
Como una Ola de Fuerza y Luz 6
Con Luigi Dallapiccola 6
Corea, Chick 19
Coro 7
Crosby, Stills, and Nash 21, 24
Crumb, George 11

Davies, Peter Maxwell 26, 27
Davis, Miles 18, 19
Death in Venice 28, 29
Deep Purple 14
Des Canyons aux Etoiles 9
Drumming 12

Dybbuk 10
Dylan, Bob 24

Eagles 21
Einstein on the Beach 12
Emerson, Lake, and Palmer 16
Eno, Brian 17, 23

Fairport Convention 21
Ferneyhough, Brian 27
Fleetwood Mac 20
Flock Descends into the Pentagonal Garden, A 9

Garner, Erroll 19
Genesis 17
Glass, Philip 4, 12
Grand Macabre, Le 9

Harry, Debbie 23
Heliogabalus Imperator 7
Henze, Hans Werner 7
Hubbard, Freddie 19

Ice Break, The 27
Inori 8

Jarrett, Keith 18
Jethro Tull 17
John, Elton 25

King, Carole 4
Kiss 15
Knot Garden, The 27

Led Zeppelin 14
Lennon, John 25
Ligeti, György 9
Liturgy of St. John Chrysostom 27

Mahavishnu Orchestra 19
Marley, Bob 5, 23
Martyrdom of St. Magnus, The 26

Mask of Orpheus, The 26
Mass 10
McCartney, Paul 25
McLaughlin, John 19
Menuhin, Yehudi 9
Messiaen, Olivier 9
Midsummer Marriage, The 27
Mirror on Which to Dwell, A 11
Mitchell, Joni 24
Moody Blues 17
Music for Eighteen Musicians 12
Music for Mallet Instruments, Voices, and Organ 12

Nancarrow, Conlon 10, 11
Nono, Luigi 6

Oldfield, Mike 13
Opera 7
Owen Wingrave 28
Owl and the Pussycat, The 4

Pears, Peter 28, 29
Pentangle 21
Peterson, Oscar 19
Phaedra 28
Pink Floyd 17
Pop, Iggy 17
Presley, Elvis 20

Ramones 23
Reed, Lou 17
Reich, Steve 12, 13
Riley, Terry 12, 13
Roxy Music 17
Rzewski, Frederic 6

Santana 19
Satyagraha 12
Sex Pistols 22, 23
Shaker Loops 13

Shankar, Ravi 9
Shorter, Wayne 18, 19
Shostakovich, Dmitri 28, 29
Silbury Air 26
Sofferte Onde Serene 6
Songfest 10
Spectrum 19
Stockhausen, Karlheinz 8, 13
Stone Litany 26
Streisand, Barbra 4
Symphony of Three Orchestras 11
Syringa 11

Takemitsu, Toru 9
Talking Heads 23
Tapestry 4
Tatum, Art 19
Tavener, John 27
Testimony 29
Tippett, Michael 27
Trans 8
Transit 27
Tribute to Jack Johnson, A 18
Triumph of Time, The 26
Tubular Bells 13

Ultimos Ritos 27

Vox Balaenae 11

Weather Report 18
Westerlings 26
Wings 25
Winsboro Cotton Mill Blues 6

Y Entonces Comprendió 6
Yes 16
Young, La Monte 12, 13
Young, Neil 21, 24

Zawinul, Joe 18